PURCHASE FIRST, CONSTRUCT LATER

How Procurement Entrepreneurs Excel In Business Startup Arena

Jason G. Linder

TABLE OF CONTENTS

INTRODUCTION

One of the best methods to expand your business or begin your own venture is to purchase a firm. The act of buying something for use in the manufacture of another good or service, or to sell again, is known as purchasing in business. Frequently, the first images that come to mind when someone says they want to work for themselves are cash-strapped 80-hour workweeks and the high failure rate of establishing a firm from scratch. But this is not the only approach to launch your own firm. Allowing someone else to put in those early hours and validate the idea before assuming their position has great advantages.

The decision to buy a business is a significant one, but when you do so, you have the chance to start a small business without beginning from zero and become an entrepreneur. More than 500,000 businesses exchange hands each year, and as the baby boomer generation starts retiring and selling their companies, that figure is anticipated to soar over the coming years.

Because it allows you to avoid some of the difficulties and expenses associated with launching a new business, purchasing an established business is so popular. However, the process from locating a firm for sale to finalizing the acquisition can be drawn out and challenging. Find out all you need to know before starting the process of purchasing your own company to prevent experiencing buyer's regret.

Purchasing an existing company has a number of benefits over creating your own. You save time, obviously. Let's say you wish to launch a retail company. It can take you several months to compile a sufficient inventory. Building a manufacturing company from the ground up might take years; opening your own restaurant requires developing your own menus and recipes. The "dirty work" has already been done, though, if you buy an existing company.

If the company you wish to purchase provides either a product or a service, you can assess its working history and have a deeper understanding of the established market. Do consumers purchase the good or service? What are they prepared to spend? What kind of advertising has shown to be most successful? Identifying your market can take years of trial and error when you first launch your own firm. A corporate acquisition can speed up this procedure.

By purchasing an established company, you will be able to assess its cash flow and running costs, which will help you determine how much investment capital you will require. These figures are more harder to calculate when you start your own business, and investors view start-up companies as being riskier than those with established operating histories and successful track records.

The potential of the existing firm is arguably the biggest benefit of purchasing over beginning a new venture. You might have a stronger business plan than the present owner, or you might see prospects for expansion that they don't. Your passion and love for the company can reenergize it and spur growth, and frequently only a few little adjustments to procedures, staff, or advertising can have a significant impact on profitability.

CHAPTER 1

THE ENTREPRENEURIAL MINDSET

An entrepreneurial mentality is a group of assumptions, mental models, and worldviews that motivate entrepreneurial activity. Entrepreneurs typically have a strong belief that they can better their lives and live on own terms. They also have confidence in their capacity to succeed and learn, develop, and adapt.

In spite of the circumstances, an entrepreneurial mindset is flexible, resilient, adaptable, resourceful, and solutions-focused. These mindsets produce lifelong learners who are creative and curious as well as critical thinkers.

Entrepreneurship fosters innovation, creates jobs, stimulates economies, and provides answers to a variety of societal and environmental problems. Entrepreneurs have tenacity and creativity. When the rules are unclear and the way is unclear, they are innovative and critical thinkers who can identify opportunities, gather support, and bring about change. Simply said, they have the character attributes and education that the modern world demands. They are the global forerunners of innovation and development.

It takes creativity and innovation to think like an entrepreneur. Entrepreneurship, at its core, is a process through which a person or small group of people look for the point at where their interests and skills meet the needs of others. Therefore, we must reframe entrepreneurship as the independent pursuit of chances to add value for others. This definition can be accepted by everyone. What can we do to make our skills more valuable to more people is the question we should all be asking ourselves. How might entrepreneurial thought influence the world for the better?

The majority of business owners combine risk aversion with creative zeal while establishing their companies. According to the debate in this chapter, early-stage entrepreneurs struggle with a lack of resources, which limits their ability to translate ideas into profitable ventures and maintain autocracy in the workplace environment. Entrepreneurs frequently face psychological obstacles brought on by knowledge gaps as well as distinctions in culture, language, educational systems, and levels of economic development. Small business operations might be hampered by even something as simple as having to accommodate the varying workweek arrangements around the world. The chapter's topic includes maps the attitude of entrepreneurs in managing opportunities and problems both inside and outside the company. It also covers the new cognitive push for new businesses and international start-ups as a strategy to compete with more established, larger competitors while utilizing significantly fewer resources. This chapter covers topics such as entrepreneurship development, entrepreneurial thought processes, and managing the learning curve in addition to the cognitive characteristics of entrepreneurs.

When you consider it, the value of having an entrepreneurial attitude becomes clear. Because they think, behave, and experience the world differently than other people, entrepreneurs are successful in the ways that they are.

The value of having an entrepreneurial attitude cannot be overstated. For instance, fostering an entrepreneurial mindset can aid in lowering worry, fear, and doubt. It may also encourage movement, concentration, and development. To put it simply, having an entrepreneurial mindset is the key to company success.

SETTING A GOAL

Setting goals is the act of determining the precise, quantifiable, doable, pertinent, and time-bound objectives that a person or organization wishes to accomplish. It entails determining the desired effects and creating a strategy for obtaining them.

Setting entrepreneur goals is the process through which company experts set detailed goals for the future. These might be both short-term and long-term goals. Entrepreneurs can set attainable objectives when starting a new firm to help them succeed.

It's critical to establish your business goals, especially before you launch, if you're serious about making a success of your venture. The ability to act however they like, whenever they please, without interference from others, is the ideal for some people. Others are aiming for financial security.

Setting goals as an entrepreneur is crucial since it takes time, perseverance, and passion to launch a successful firm. Whether you're starting a new business or growing an existing one, setting goals can help you monitor your success. Setting goals aids in improving your ability to visualize your ideas and thoughts. Planning ahead will allow you to make the necessary adjustments at each stage of your entrepreneurial journey, which could increase productivity.

Today's environment is one where competition is getting progressively more intense. You will fall behind if you can't adjust, prioritize, and accomplish tasks more quickly than your rivals. Setting, concentrating on, and achieving goals is a key component of being a successful entrepreneur.

Specifications of Your Goals
Specificity: If a goal is defined, you have a better probability of accomplishing it. Raising $10,000 by July 1 is the target; raising cash is not.
Optimism: When you set your goals, think positively. Paying the bills isn't exactly an inspiring objective. Having financial security frames your goal more positively, igniting your motivation to pursue it.

Realism: Setting a monthly income goal of $100,000 when you've never made that much in a year is unrealistic. Start out by making little changes, like raising your monthly salary by 25%. You can aim for bigger goals once you've accomplished your first one.

Long and short duration: Short-term objectives can be completed in a few weeks to a year. Long-term objectives should be significantly more ambitious than short-term objectives while still being feasible; they can be for five, ten, or even twenty years.

1. Establish goals: After deciding on the type of business you want to launch, you may start drafting a list of objectives. Make sure each objective is reasonable, detailed, and actionable. Depending on the nature of your business enterprise, you may select several objectives. You might decide to sell 100 goods in the first month if you are establishing a sales company, for instance.

2. Ask Why: Setting a goal is one thing; pursuing it and making it happen is quite another. The many reasons you desire to accomplish your objective and make it a reality are listed in the big why. The car's fuel is what powers it along. Most people overlook this phase, which prevents them from succeeding in their goals.

3. Specify due dates: Setting timelines for your goals after you've established them is beneficial. For your company, deadlines might produce a precise schedule. You can utilize this deadline, for instance, to make sure your firm launches on time if you want it to do so in four months.

4. Writing: List the actions you must do to accomplish the goal in writing. After that, list the actions for each goal. Every step you must take to accomplish each objective on your list should be precisely defined. Try to break down each significant objective into doable chores. You can use this to develop a workable plan. If you are part of a team, include any suggestion you and your colleagues have that will enable you to accomplish your main objective. Then, you should group them into appropriate task groups that you or your team can successfully execute.

5. Set the steps' priority: You can organize and prioritise these jobs once you have established stages for each objective. Think about the desired sequencing of the tasks. For instance, you might need to get in touch with your target market initially if you want to bring in 10 new clients in your first month of operation.

6. List the challenges to the goal: Identifying the challenges you can encounter is one of the finest strategies to manage your goals. You can better prepare for overcoming hurdles by defining prospective ones. You have a better chance of saving time and priceless resources the more equipped you are to deal with problems.

7. Take initiative: You can start acting now that your goals have been established. To assist you get closer to your goals, try to work on a tiny job or step each day. Think about scheduling regular goal reviews. As your company expands, this might assist you in making modifications.

CHAPTER 2

FINDING OPPORTUNITIES

Purchasing an existing company can reduce the amount of time spent waiting for a paycheck, lessen the financial burden of starting a new company, creating markets, and other start-up expenses. Intangible assets like historical value or reputation are examples of good will that established businesses may already possess. A pre-owned business purchase needs careful consideration of a number of variables, including financing and cost. You need to be aware of the standards used to choose a company.

While starting from scratch normally entails higher upfront costs, buying an existing company usually carries lower risks. Financially, you're examining actual profit and loss records rather than educated guesses, and you can reference a transparent sales history. Additionally, you could be able to secure priceless patents or copyrights, as well as have the chance to use your talents to steer a stale organization in an exhilarating route.

The following inquiries need to be taken into account:
• Is the place desirable?
• Can you secure the necessary funding?
• Does the company's strengths align with yours?
• How long have you worked in this field?
• How much money are you prepared to put up?
• Do you think you would enjoy working in this line of work?
• Is the company making money?
What size organization do you want in terms of personnel, sales, and profits?
• What makes customers value the company?
• Is the good or service distinct from others on the market?
• What is the culture of the business?
• Do you have sufficient knowledge of the company or sector?
• Do you have any unaccounted-for expenses?

1. Choose your search criteria: A major choice that will affect your life and means of support for many years is buying a business. Therefore, start by clearly defining the type of business you're searching for before you even begin evaluating your possibilities.

2. Examine the accessible companies: You'll need to start looking into firms that are for sale once you've decided what you're looking for.

Start by making some inquiries close to home. Are your pals who recently released a popular software prepared to start working on their next endeavor? Do you work for a small company you adore, whose owners could be interested in selling? Or, if you prefer to keep things small and local, perhaps the proprietors of your preferred neighborhood coffee shop are prepared to sell up and relocate to Bermuda? It doesn't hurt to inquire if you are aware of a company that you would want to own. From there, go out to your contacts in business and cautiously use the internet for research. A reputable internet marketplace for buying businesses is BizBuySell. But take caution—for every genuine opportunity that may be found online, there are others of scams just waiting to happen.

3. Take into account using a company broker: Consider working with a business broker to prescreen potential businesses for you, assist you identify your areas of interest, and negotiate the terms of your final business purchase if you've done some independent research and haven't discovered the company you're searching for.

Similar to real estate agents, business brokers are paid only when you purchase a business and normally charge a commission of between 5 and 10 percent of the acquisition price. Therefore, even though using a broker's help may be worthwhile, exercise caution and resist the need to make a snap decision.

4. Complete your research: A true entrepreneur will be eager to buy a firm and take it to the next level as soon as they find one that's a suitable fit. Do your homework and take things gently before you become overly enthused. A company that appears to be doing well on the surface can actually be masking some serious problems, making it a poor candidate for sale. Get your acquisitions team organized before moving on. You will require the assistance of an acquisitions lawyer and an independent business valuations firm to ascertain the worth and viability of the company, particularly if you are not working with a broker.

Have a business appraisal done to ascertain the company's value, and take into account how the present owner's connections and experience may impact that value. A business sale, for instance, could result in the clients of the prior owner leaving a business-to-business organization, which would have a significant negative effect on the value of the company. Have a qualified accountant thoroughly review the company's written financials to ensure everything is in order and to raise any doubts about anything that may be confusing. Don't leave anything to chance since when you purchase a business, you assume a lot of responsibility for events that may have occurred before you were engaged.

If you play your cards right, buying an existing business may be a great investment for a number of compelling reasons. But bear in mind that you'll be continuing the legacy of the previous owner, so you need to be knowledgeable about every aspect of the business you're about to buy.

Before making a purchase decision, you should consider the advantages and disadvantages of doing so.

Advantages of buying an existing business

- It might be a quicker way to launch a company.
- Systems and practices are in place. A portion of the groundwork needed to establish the firm will have already been done.
- You are aware of the business's financial history.The company's track record and likelihood of success may make financing more accessible.
- A market for the good or service will already have been established.

- You have clients or customers. There might be a consistent flow of clients, consistent income, a strong reputation to build on, and a useful network of contacts.
- A business plan and marketing strategy have to be in place already.
- You ought to be able to benefit from the expertise of current employees. A group of knowledgeable, skilled workers are at your disposal.
- Many of the problems will have already been located and dealt with.
- You might have only one place or several.
- Less risk exists. You might be able to persuade the seller to finance it given that it has a good reputation, is currently in business, has clients and customers, employees, systems, suppliers, a financial history, and a location or locations.

Disadvantages of buying an existing business

- You typically need to make a substantial initial investment in addition to budgeting money for professional charges like accountants, surveyors, and other specialists.

- You'll likely also need working capital, which is the amount needed to cover expenses for several months, to help with cash flow.
- If it has been disregarded, you might need to invest much more money than the acquisition price in order to offer the company the best chance of success.
- You may need to uphold any unresolved contracts from the previous owner or renegotiate them.
- In addition, you should consider any potential consequences for the business and your takeover, as well as the reason the current owner is selling up.
- It's possible that current workers are dissatisfied with their new manager or that low employee morale is a result of the company's poor management.

Other things to note:

1. Marketing tactics and expenditures for advertising: What kinds of marketing tactics have been successful in the past? It's crucial that you learn the statistics for each channel. What were the figures for the cost per acquisition? How much was spent on each channel on average? What kinds of creatives succeeded or failed? Which strategy was most successful? You will waste time and efforts if you don't find out this information in advance.

2. Accounting Records: It makes sense to enlist the help of an accountant at this point. Request financial records from the past five years and use reports from websites like Dun & Bradstreet(www.dnb.com) to compare the figures/ratios with industry norms. Obtain all P&L and balance sheet data as well as any other relevant information.

3. Incorporation: If your business is incorporated, be sure to find out where state it is registered in and whether it is conducting business within its own state as a foreign corporation.

4. Contracts and legal paperwork: All contracts pertaining to partnerships, leases and purchases, subcontractors, sales, employment agreements, and other legal matters should be stored safely. Bring in an attorney to help you review the documentation if you have any questions.

5. Sales statistics: To get a clear picture of how the company operates, look for sales data from the last five years and pay attention to each category. Analyze the top 10–20 accounts for the past year or two and compare the numbers to those in the sector. To guide your judgments, you're searching for rates (percentages) and trends.

6. A list of obligations: Exist any assets subject to liens? Lawsuits? Any other assertions? To help you with this, get an accountant and an attorney. If not, there can be legal repercussions.

7. The brand's reputation: What do customers have to say? Try searching "[company] scam" to see what results you get. Investigate more to discover the true narrative. For a quick reputation check, you can even just Google the company.

8. All due and receivable balances: Request a list of all accounts receivable and payable that are 90 days or older. If a client is blatantly taking advantage of you with respect to receivables (for instance, by delaying payment past 90 days), you should think about ending the relationship. For both pages, make a list of your "top 10" clientele.

9. Relationships between sellers and buyers: Exist any clients having unique connections to the vendor. Is there a specific bargain that you might not be aware of with a certain customer group. When the business is acquired, would these customers still make purchases?

10. Payroll: Look for any inflated salaries by analyzing all of the present salaries. Pay attention to salaries for those who do not actively contribute to the company (such as family).

11. Place and market region: This isn't a major issue for online enterprises. Everything in retail enterprises revolves around location. Take a stroll around the neighborhood on your own to observe the nearby businesses, the local populace, and your overall impression of the location.

12. An org chart and a list of the current staff: You need to be aware of who is in charge of what and who reports to whom. In order to audit the business procedures, if available, request access to the internal wiki or documentation.

13. Protection: Is the company fully insured? What kind of insurance, if any, is covered, and what are the premiums for?

14. Product returns: What is the return rate as a percentage? per item or service? How do the return rates measure up to the averages for the sector?

15. Consumer trends: Is the company a seasonal one? Do particular client groups favor particular products? How are they ejected? Your learning process will be sped up by any form of learned patterns.

Making A Transaction

For entrepreneurs, negotiation and deal-making abilities are essential. Success depends not just on brilliant concepts and effective marketing techniques, but also on a network of agreements that all business owners must establish. Deals with staff, manufacturing, distribution, marketing, and funding are a few of these. Not to mention the exit agreement, which is intended to make all of that work and the other deals profitable at the end of the cycle. When a huge deal is being closed, it's simple to make a mistake.

- Prospect, create a pipeline, and be everywhere at once.
- Express yourself clearly, firmly, and favorably.
- Bargain, don't cut corners, and take your time.
- Keep in mind that refusing a deal can result in even greater ones.

1.Know your worth: You need to have a firm understanding of the value of your company before engaging in any negotiations. You can estimate your valuation using a variety of techniques, including revenue multiples, discounted cash flow, and market comparables. Additionally, you want to think about your capacity for expansion, comparative advantage, clientele, and intellectual property. Setting your expectations and supporting your asking price will be made easier if you have a reasonable and defendable valuation.

2.Negotiate your terms: You must do this once you have found a potential buyer and have received a preliminary offer. This covers the purchase price, the method of payment, the date of closure, the warranties, and the contingencies. You should be ready to give certain things up while simultaneously maintaining your non-negotiables. Additionally, you ought to be prepared to back out of a contract if it's not in your best interests. To assist you with the legal, financial, and practical sides of the deal, you should work with a broker, an accountant, and a lawyer.

3.Get ready: Being well-prepared may enable you to develop your plan before to the negotiation itself. Additionally, it implies that you are better prepared to deal with unforeseen developments at any point in the negotiation process. Knowing what you want from the negotiation, what your opponent wants, and what your leverages are is the first step in effective preparation. Try to comprehend the implications of a certain contract for your company in general and your individual business unit; the risks involved, the rewards if you succeed, and the consequences if you fail. This would provide a solid indication of your motivators, strengths, and leverages.

Finding your USP (Unique Selling Point), understanding how it helps the customer, and how it differentiates you from the competitors are all effective ways to increase leverage. Knowing the risks and leverages can help you evaluate your leverage over the opposing party and start the negotiation process with greater assurance.

4.Play to your strengths, but watch out for your flaws: It's possible that you don't fully comprehend and know the opponent's strategy. However, you may and should evaluate your own talents and use them to your advantage as well as recognize and effectively address any flaws.

You may better grasp where you stand with the client and in comparison to your competition by being aware of your own strengths and limitations. This information will not only offer you an edge over your competitors, but it will also provide you significant negotiating power with the customer.

5.Understand what the other side desires: The best leverage is information. Particularly when it comes to understanding what the other party (the customer, supplier, etc.) expects from the transaction. Understanding this is just as important as understanding your own wants and advantages. It is possible to properly portray yourself as the best or the preferred alternative in the market after you have a solid understanding of what the other party anticipates from the transaction.

You will have more negotiating power if you have more knowledge, such as alternatives to the good or service being discussed. Of course, a lot of the information would be private and unavailable to the public. But if you do your homework, you can always find enough information that is already in the public domain or that the other party has shared, utilizing which you can get a good notion of what their needs are, the stakes involved, and their leverages.

CHAPTER THREE

BUILDING YOUR BUSINESS

As a purpose-driven entrepreneur, your major goal is to build a successful business and improve the world. In the modern world, consumers are becoming more aware of their impact on the environment and society, which has raised demand for businesses with a purpose.

1. Determining your objective: The driving force behind achieving your company's goals. It serves as both the impetus for your brand and the reason you founded your business. Every decision you make as a purpose-driven entrepreneur must support the goals of your business.

When deciding what you want your purpose to be, consider the impact you want to have on society and the environment. Once you've chosen your purpose, make sure to include it in every aspect of your business, including your mission statement, branding, and service or product offerings.

2. Get prepared: To flourish as a business owner, you must be well-organized. You will be able to do tasks fast and keep track of the numerous tasks that need to be completed thanks to this. A simple way to get and keep organized is to create a to-do list every day. As you complete each item on your list, cross it off. Remember that certain tasks are more important than others as well. Prioritize finishing the most crucial activities first.

3. Formulating a long-term business plan: A sustainable business model is essential in purpose-driven entrepreneurship, which aspires to achieve long-term financial, societal, and environmental sustainability. This makes it possible to strike a balance between social issues and economic development, while also taking environmental implications into consideration and making sure the company generates value for its owners.

Use renewable resources to reduce waste and carbon footprints in this strategy. Select environmentally friendly transportation options, such as bicycles or electric cars. Instead of using conventional energy sources, think about using green energy and energy-saving technologies. Use recyclable or biodegradable packaging whenever possible.

4. Examine Your Competition: If you want to succeed, you cannot afford to ignore your competitors. Spend your time studying them and learning from them instead. The cost of acquiring this kind of competition intelligence is high for larger companies.

There may be several methods for competitor analysis, depending on your company's needs. If you run a restaurant or retail location, you might be able to learn more about your competitors by simply dining or buying there, then asking customers what they like or dislike about it.

5. Assessing your impact: Making a business with a purpose requires measuring your impact. Observe your development, identify your weak points, and persuade others to respect your authority. Decide on distinct KPI sets that are in line with your target statement.

Environmental or social audits can help identify issue areas, track change across time, and guide more effective CSR activities. You can also utilize evaluation techniques like the B Impact evaluation, the B Corp accreditation, or the Sustainable Development Goals (SDGs) to assess your company's sustainability impact and set goals for improvement.

6. Collaborate with other mission-driven businesses: Because it helps you to connect with other groups that share your aims and have a greater impact, collaboration is a crucial aspect of purpose-driven business. Use best practices, share key lessons learned, and cooperate to generate new ideas in order to achieve your business goals.

Working together is a terrific way to bring a variety of perspectives and skill sets to the table and promote your company at the same time. Find organizations that are comparable to your own and cooperate together on initiatives like joint marketing campaigns, networking events, and CSR initiatives. It will also strengthen the goals and objectives of your company while having a long-lasting impact on society.

7. Remain adaptable and imaginative: Entrepreneurship with a goal necessitates a creative and adaptable mindset. In order to adapt to the quickly changing business environment, identify new opportunities for innovation, and follow current trends, entrepreneurs must be adaptable. When evaluating your business model and strategies on a frequent basis, keep the newest emerging trends and technologies in mind.

8. Understand the Benefits and Risks: Another crucial element of success is the capacity to take calculated risks in order to progress your business. Along with considering the potential benefits if you are successful, it is a good idea to consider "What's the downside if this doesn't work out?". If you can answer that question, you can figure out the worst-case scenario. If you think you could handle that chance and are prepared to take the necessary precautions to reduce the danger, you might want to give it a try. If not, this could be a good time to consider other options. Understanding risks and rewards is necessary to make informed decisions about when to launch a new product or start a new business. As an illustration, the massive economic disruption caused by the COVID outbreak gave rise to both new opportunities for some firms, such as those who produce and sell protective gear, as well as difficult obstacles for others, such as those that run restaurants with indoor dining limitations.

9. Be Innovative: Constantly explore for ways to improve your business and make it stand out from the crowd. Recognize your limitations and be open to trying new things. Watch for opportunities to expand your current firm or establish affiliated ventures that will boost revenue and profit from diversity.

10. Be Trustworthy: Consistency is the key to business success. To succeed, you must continually do the appropriate actions. This will create long-lasting positive attitudes that will allow you to earn money over time and attract satisfied customers right away. Additionally, customers value consistency.

11. Make yourself more visible online: Even if you don't own an online business, expanding your online brand presence is crucial to getting your product in front of more consumers, especially if it sells directly to them.

Financing Your Business

Individual Savings: You should start with your own equity or assets while looking for money. Personal resources include items like real estate equity loans, cash value insurance policies, profit-sharing or early retirement funds. You put up some of your own money as collateral for the loan, either in the form of cash or an asset. This will demonstrate to your banker that you are committed to your project over the long term.

Family and Friends: A startup company's founders could ask their parents or friends for private financing. If it comes in the form of equity capital, the friend or family would then receive ownership in the company. However, these transactions should be conducted with the same formality as would be used with outside investors.

Enterprise Angels: These are the professional investors who contribute some or all of their financial resources to the expansion of creative businesses, in addition to their time. According to reports, angel investments are three times larger than venture capital investments. Angel investors are wealthy people or former corporate leaders who make direct investments in startups that are already owned by others. They are typically acknowledged as leading authorities in their disciplines and offer not just their extensive network of contacts and knowledge, but also their technical and/or managerial know-how.

During a startup's early stages, angel investors often invest between $25,000 and $100,000. Institutional venture investors want investments that are no more than $1 million. They take a financial risk in exchange for the chance to examine the organization's management techniques. For instance, this often denotes a commitment to openness and a position on the board of directors.

Venture capital: The most important thing to keep in mind is that not all business owners will undoubtedly profit from this type of investment. You should be aware that venture capitalists are seeking technology-driven businesses and organizations with significant growth potential in industries like biotechnology, communications, and information technology.

In order to support the company's execution of a promising but riskier idea, venture capitalists invest in it by purchasing shares. This entails giving a third party a stake in your firm in exchange for a piece of the ownership or stock. Venture investors also expect to recoup a sizable portion of their initial investment once the company begins offering shares to the general public. Make careful to seek out investors who have the skills and expertise your company requires. The financial investor in this kind of corporate financing buys a stake in the startup company in exchange for capital and financial guidance. Therefore, venture capitalists seek out businesses with strong growth prospects, outstanding management teams, and low leverage potential.

Loans and Overdraft s: A long-term method of financing entrepreneurial endeavors is through bank loans. The overdraft facility is only momentarily available. The financial institution must state the duration of the loan, as well as the amount, frequency, and interest rate. For the bank loan, the business owner offers some form of security. It is the best option for financing investments in fixed assets. When compared to a bank overdraft, they provide a reduced interest rate. They perform poorly, nevertheless, when it comes to adaptability.

If an entrepreneur's bank balance is insufficient, a bank overdraft may be helpful. They can also directly borrow money from the bank and pay a high interest rate. Therefore, they are perfect for controlling seasonal swings in cash flow or when a company experiences a temporary liquidity problem.

Buyouts: This type of corporate financing has the power to change a company's ownership structure. The primary objective of a buyout is still to increase the company's value once it becomes a private company and is freed from the regulatory obligations that come with being a publicly traded company. The buyout endeavor may need the sale of non-core assets, concentration on the company's objective, streamlining of procedures, updating of product lines, and removal of the existing management, among other things.

Federal assistance: The federal and state governments commonly offer startup or emerging firms financial support in the form of grants or tax credits. Governmental organizations aid Canadian businesses because it's not always simple to spread inventions. This money might go toward paying for things like marketing, salaries, R&D, equipment, and productivity enhancement.

A grant, in the strictest sense, is a sum of money that is handed to your business with the understanding that you will not be compelled to repay it. The grant must be used in line with the terms of the agreement; otherwise, you can be required to repay the funds. Furthermore, it is normal to acquire additional financing from a government source after receiving assistance from that source in the past if you match the program's conditions.

Assembling The Right Team

Every leader needs to create their own support network, which is the first and most crucial network to do so. A competent leadership team consists of both internal managers and external consultants that can assist the leader in maintaining perspective, spotting excellent possibilities, and carrying out crucial ideas.

Being an entrepreneur might be difficult, but the best way to succeed is to assemble a solid, viable, creative team with a wide range of talents that can benefit your company. Keep it compact, independent, adaptable, coherent, and reliable.

Putting a team together from current employees and employing new people to design and launch a new firm or business prospect have a lot in common. Selecting individuals with compatible work ethics will benefit your company.

On first glance, building a strong team doesn't seem like a very difficult undertaking. We frequently believe that if we gather a team of hard-working, like-minded people, we will be successful. Forming a team, however, does not ensure performance, and using outdated team management techniques can lead to the failure of your team or your project.

1.Begin with you: To avoid seeming corny, I'll say this: Self-awareness is the cornerstone of all virtue. You are the foundation of a strong team. Here's the evidence: The truth is that you won't possess every single competency required to scale a startup. First, assess your skill set objectively. What do you excel at? What are you missing? Additionally, it goes beyond only hard talents. The soft characteristics also have a role. Up to 77% of employers concur that soft skills are equally crucial. You need to consider factors like your personality, your values, and your views. When you fully understand what you contribute to the table, you can begin to consider your team. Practice what you excel at. Find capable people to take care of the rest.

2. Keep it small: Pick a small group of people who have a variety of skills and are willing to listen to different points of view. This structure enables team members to collaborate closely and develop deep relationships. The team must work well together and value working as a unit. They should enjoy spending time working together and be able to constructively criticize each other's ideas while still moving the task ahead.

3. Establish quantifiable goals: As a leader, you should establish goals that are both clear and measurable in order to keep the team on task and to hold individuals responsible for their work. Accountability fosters loyalty, boosts morale, and ensures your team's trust in you. It also keeps teams on target.

4. Demand or ask for self-sufficiency: Although it may be challenging, always employ people who are capable of acting independently.

People who can see beyond the task at hand and consider all of the possible outcomes are what you desire. The team should be given a mission and then be free to devise strategies, utilize resources, and manage their time as they see fit.

5. Remain adaptable: Because they are working under less restrictions, teams that are flexible and allowed to experiment and explore new ideas before developing the final product or proposal are more likely to succeed. We have always done it this way is one thing that should not be said. Each trial run must be improved upon and refined by the team.

6. Rely on your network: It's not always simple to find the ideal teammate. Let your personal and professional networks know the type of individual you're searching for, as networking is a tried-and-true method of finding new hires. Then set up one-on-one introductions, plan a meeting to determine the candidate's fit with the team, and take them out to lunch with the present team to see how they get along.

7. Choose team members that share your values: Once you have a senior management team in place, the following stage is to build a positive culture by selecting people who have the correct motivation and objectives. Make sure the people you hire share the same passions as you.

8: Character matters: To hire team members who don't get along is a surefire way to destroy your startup. Work that must be done will be impeded by ongoing conflict. I'm not advocating that a specific personality quirk should be a requirement to join your team. In fact, a diverse group is what you want. However, you ought to get to know your group. What qualities do they have? You can tell if someone will fit well on your team based on these characteristics. But creating a team that will function successfully as a unit is only one aspect. That's a sizable portion of it, but there are also other essential factors to take into account. What objectives do the members of your team have? How does the job fit into these objectives? I'll explain why that's significant. Not everyone applying for jobs at your company is in it for the long run. It might not be their final goal, but it can help them get closer to it. For instance, someone might wish to join your team so they can network and build relationships. Do you think you shouldn't hire them in light of that? It's up to you to decide that. Even if it's only for a short duration, they can still be useful to your company. However, if you want people who will consistently provide excellent work, make sure that their objectives line up with the position. The most crucial factor is that you be aware of the goals of your team members.

CHAPTER FOUR

SCALING AND SUSTAINING

Businesses frequently find novel ways to carry out specific tasks as they expand in order to retain productivity and maintain profitability. In order to lower risk and get the organization ready to better manage its expansion, leadership teams can build and test these new processes or procedures by scaling a firm. You can build a company that will be successful in the long run by comprehending how this process works.

Business leadership teams must scale their operations to assure growth without compromising quality or raising prices. A business that has effectively expanded has the infrastructure to manage rising sales volumes while steadily cutting expenses. By successfully planning and preparing systems, employees, and processes for sustainable long-term growth and profitability, businesses may support growth. Scaling is the ability of a developing business to guarantee economical output and a productive workforce.

1. Create a solid plan: Planning is not the enemy when stepping away from your safety net. Contrarily, it is crucial. In fact, it takes new or alternative plans to pivot successfully from existing ones. That is accurate for company strategic scaling. As you scale up, having a plan of action will make it simpler to maintain your high performance standards and introduce additional operations while lowering your exposure to risks and losses. Finding all of the potential obstacles to your growth is a smart place to start so you can plan how to get around or over them. When scaling, it's critical to take into account your product offerings, marketing, finance sources, internal procedures, workforce, physical location of your firm, and infrastructure in addition to revenue growth. Consider exploring ways to expand the operational capability of your business so that it can manage extra sales or work without affecting current operations. Creating a well-organized, adaptive, and durable strategy is the objective, and having a solid plan can help you achieve your objectives.

2. Obtain funding: Scaling a business before seeing an increase in sales can be expensive, but if you created a solid business plan, you can obtain finance that contributes to the success of the company. Consider a variety of choices when looking for new financial prospects, including equity financing with angel or venture capitalists, crowdsourcing, debt financing through loans or a line of credit, and more. It's crucial to plan out how much money you want to invest and how you'll spend it.

3. Define realistic and specific goals: Try to define objectives for every aspect of your firm, including revenue growth, cost control, hiring and training new employees, and staff recruiting and development. Each team member can better understand their position in the growth and the company's future by developing a business plan for expansion with clear benchmarks for success in all areas. To track progress and add more milestones, think about combining short- and long-term objectives when making goals. Setting attainable goals can guarantee that you don't scale your firm too quickly. In many cases, steady, sustained growth is better for a company than sudden overexpansion.

4. Know what your customers want: Your buyer personas must be able to respond to the following inquiries in order to properly comprehend what your customers actually want:

- Who arc your clients?
- How do they behave?
- Why are they purchasing?
- When do they purchase?
- How do they purchase?
- What are they making?
- Why are they buying?
- How do they perceive you?
- How do people feel about your rivals?
- What do people anticipate of you?

Your staff will be able to comprehend what your customer actually wants thanks to these crucial points. Additionally, it's a good idea to consider your company's expansion from the viewpoint of your clients. Your internal team needs to be focused and set goals for your company's success.

5. Modify the internal organization: As your company grows, you may wish to hire additional workers, and a hands-on approach where you know every employee may not be feasible in a larger company. As your firm expands, it's crucial to make sure new hires contribute to upholding your core principles. Try to foster an atmosphere and culture where people desire to work and succeed, as this can aid in keeping them properly engaged and motivated. When recruiting new employees, keep in mind creating and expressing the company's values. By asking them to specify what's most important to them and making sure everyone in the organization understands how the firm runs, you can also involve current employees. Scalability is aided by a strong sense of corporate identity.

6. Networking and Collaboration: The philosophy that encourages expansion and scalability must encompass partnerships and collaborations outside the boundaries of the company. The secret to long-term success is building a strong PR network. You should establish a network of partnerships with individuals and groups, including service providers, sales partners, suppliers, and customers, as they may be willing to help you by offering crucial market data. Scalability becomes easily attainable when such engagements take the shape of a formal alliance, which may happen.

7. Use your time wisely: The adage "time is money" is accurate when it comes to growing your business (and keeping that growth under control). Make sure that all scaling and growth-related tasks have deadlines. Unexpected pressing jobs frequently reveal themselves at the worst moments, such as during expansion and scalability. Utilize time management tools and tactics to make the most of the time you have to ensure that your team is productive throughout the growth process and can adapt to last-minute adjustments or deviations in schedules and assignments. Develop time management skills with your team. Microsoft Project, ClickUp, and TaskQue are just a few of the software and application options available to you to ensure that your business's time is used effectively. Employing a project manager could be beneficial.

8. Be familiar with your team: One benefit of increasing operations is the chance to spot weak points in your chain of command. Monitoring your team's performance while you scale is just as crucial as taking into account their feedback and suggestions for when and how to scale. It is unlikely that scaling up with a staff that is particularly resistant to change or incompetent will lead to much development; in fact, it might even be harmful. Getting to know your team better can give you insights on their capacities, skills, and character that can be helpful for decision-making regarding the future of the business and maximizing the potential of your expanding organization. You'll be in a better position to choose whether to scale and how to do it if you have a comprehensive grasp of your team, organizational principles, and consumers' expectations. An effective approach for this can be gathering anonymous feedback. It is obvious that scaling requires a broader skill set. Entrepreneurs must assemble a group of people with a variety of skills. Your crew must be aware of your company's objectives and work diligently to meet them on schedule without sacrificing quality. They must possess an exceptional skill set in order for it to be achievable.

9. Take into account the best possibilities for growth: Try to analyze all of your growth options since the quickest route to achieving your goals might not be the finest one. For instance, sales may expand quickly as a result of entering a new market, yet the additional volume may overwhelm invoicing and accounts receivable processes. You can increase revenue while still guaranteeing that your accounting procedures are effective by taking into account alternative growth strategies. Try to consider how technology, consolidation, or outsourcing might fit into your growth strategy to help you succeed in this.

10. Determine your competitive advantage: It's vital to keep in mind that many business owners give in to their own ideas of where they want their company to go when determining their competitive edge. Businesses start to comprehend their market and products more as they grow. Here's an illustration for you. At some point, the owner of a computer shop will realize that offering after-sales services is preferable for him than setting up or importing gear. The proprietor of the store will then concentrate on keeping the staff happy and become an expert in all the equipment needed to offer after-sale services rather than items.

11. Track development and modify: Constantly gauge your progress against your well-defined goals and make appropriate adjustments. Being proactive about expanding with the correct goods, procedures, and people will help you have a more seamless transition as you scale your firm. Even so, keeping track of your development can enable you to see problems earlier and come up with more efficient remedies.

Risk and Change Management

The identification and mitigation of losses is the fundamental definition of risk management. A systematic process is used by an organization to identify, assess, plan, and minimize losses.

Business is all about taking risk, according to several business owners. This is a bad idea that might only result in pain and danger. We'll try to understand risk today, as well as how an entrepreneur should approach risk management.

From a business perspective, risk is simply the possibility that, given a range of possibilities, an unpleasant outcome will actually occur. Beyond the likelihood of occuring, another aspect that is essential for comprehending risk and for identifying, classifying, and controlling it is the intensity of the unpleasant impacts of the undesirable event. An undesired event can be deemed "no risk" for administrative purposes if it is unlikely to happen or if, even if it does, there will be no negative effects.

Effective risk management improves business operations' overall effectiveness, which protects and increases the likelihood that the company will survive and grow.

Depending on how successfully we manage risks in our operations, we will be able to safeguard transactions, identify projects that are having problems, take preventive action, and avoid catastrophic events. As we improve internal communication across the organization, our teams become more focused. Our service delivery, sales, cash flows, and profitability all improve thanks to effective risk management, which also cuts down on operational waste. As a result, the company gains the trust of all its stakeholders, including its employees, customers, creditors, and suppliers. All of these will improve corporate stability and resilience, raising the possibility of further growth.

The broad phrase "change management" is used to refer to the methods that organizations employ to implement both short-term and long-term organizational change, both of which are frequently required for organizations that want to survive and succeed. In order to advance an organization, change management evaluates the stages that a corporation experiences as it develops and employs a variety of techniques that are intended to optimize resource usage, enhance corporate operations, and reallocate money as needed.

Change is one of the aspects that every entrepreneur needs to be aware of. Change is constant, just like time. Time and change are inseparable. Things also have a tendency to change as time goes on. The only change you can successfully manage is the one you start. The best you can do to combat change brought on by a few other uncontrollable variables is to manage it.

1. Setting the Scene: Before addressing dangers, managers must be able to thoroughly understand and recognize them. To do this, they must first comprehend the environment in which the threats are present. In other words, managers must identify the operating environment and potential risks for their organization. They should be knowledgeable about the responsibilities, goals, and primary objectives of their company.

2. Calculating the Loss: After completely understanding the scenario, managers should develop a list of all potential hazards. This will depend on, among other things, the organizational climate and business processes. A company that manufactures chemicals, for instance, may be at risk of leaks from its production facilities. There are four basic types of dangers. Physical risks, as the name suggests, are those that affect an organization's observable (physical) assets and outside factors. Second, there are dangers associated with money, such as paying insurance premiums, paying for losses, borrowing money, paying taxes, etc. Thirdly, it may be ethical to take chances that could harm one's reputation or values. Last but not least, laws themselves may lead to legal issues.

3. Examining and analyzing risks: Risks are present in any firm, but the possibility that they will manifest varies based on the circumstance. Managers should assess the possibility of any prospective risk materializing. This is necessary because more serious dangers must be given weight than less dangerous ones. The expense of mitigating a risk will rise as it becomes more likely to occur. Therefore, risk analysis helps to estimate how much risk mitigation will cost.

4. Handling the Risks: After identifying and analyzing the risks, managers must take the necessary steps. This process can entail totally avoiding risks. It is also possible to reduce a risk's potential negative effects. For instance, a plant may employ safety measures and equipment to prevent worker injuries. Even the transfer of risk to other organizations is an option. During this process, all potential liability to other parties is transferred using contracts and notices. For instance, shopping centers regularly transfer ownership of parked cars to the owners in the event of damage.

5. Go slowly and have realistic expectations: Change, particularly organizational change, does not happen in a vacuum, as it does with everything else in life. According to everything we've learned about change management, significant change like this shouldn't happen immediately (unless, of course, a global epidemic strikes). For any change to be effective, preparation, ensuring that staff have reasonable expectations for timeframe and execution, and having the flexibility to allow the organization to shift over time are essential.

Change Management seeks to reduce any potential problems that employees might have with a planned change by virtue of its intrinsic focus on structure and concern for everyone inside the organization. However, it goes without saying that any choice made will have repercussions across the entire organization. Therefore, any strategies that are implemented ought to have a strong emphasis on inclusivity and transparency.

The idea of change for organizations this year might be frightening, but using change management to encourage openness and transparency among employees need not be so difficult. Small adjustments made now could have a significant long-term effect. One thing that may be easily implemented into company policy is transparency, so long as it begins at the top. This could entail holding "ask me anything" sessions where staff members are given the chance to ask management questions they wouldn't typically have the chance to ask (this is crucial if they have concerns about the upcoming changes in the company and their role going forward). Business leaders can also encourage inclusivity by encouraging active listening within teams and enabling staff to participate in decision-making where appropriate. This is even remotely achievable with the use of interactive polls and surveys, all created to help leaders make better decisions that have greater support for the organization. Business executives should practice open communication and ensure that enough channels have been developed through the use of modern technologies. This applies to disseminating critical firm information, such as the acquisition of new clients or financial data. All of these modest adjustments will be quite helpful in moving the company toward more innovative and exciting working arrangements, such as totally remote or hybrid arrangements.

CONCLUSION

The best business for you to buy will rely on your needs and way of life. Make sure to take the time to investigate and comprehend the company and industry.

Purchasing an established company might have benefits. Businesses with a successful track record are more likely to know how to manage profitable operations. Additionally, it is simpler for these companies to obtain bank financing.
You can establish your own business without having to overcome the numerous challenges associated with starting from scratch by purchasing an existing company. But that does not imply that purchasing a firm is simple. This path is lengthy, difficult, and rife with possible

snags. Some phases can endure for more than a year.

Established firms can, however, also have drawbacks. You may have to deal with unfinished contracts in this category or a bad reputation that the former owner left behind.

It's crucial to conduct study to make sure your choice is the appropriate one. You must investigate the company's books, strategies, and operations while becoming knowledgeable about your rivals and the sector.

In order to guide you through the procedure, you should think about speaking with a business advisor.

Be sure to conduct thorough research before thinking about purchasing a business. Understanding the reputation and potential of the company you intend to purchase will be possible thanks to your research. To avoid any costly shocks after the sale, you must conduct as much research as you can about the company during the buying process.

You can better understand a company's clients and the market it competes in by conducting market research.

To obtain a sense of how the company is doing, you could also want to speak with its current clients, staff members, and neighboring business owners.